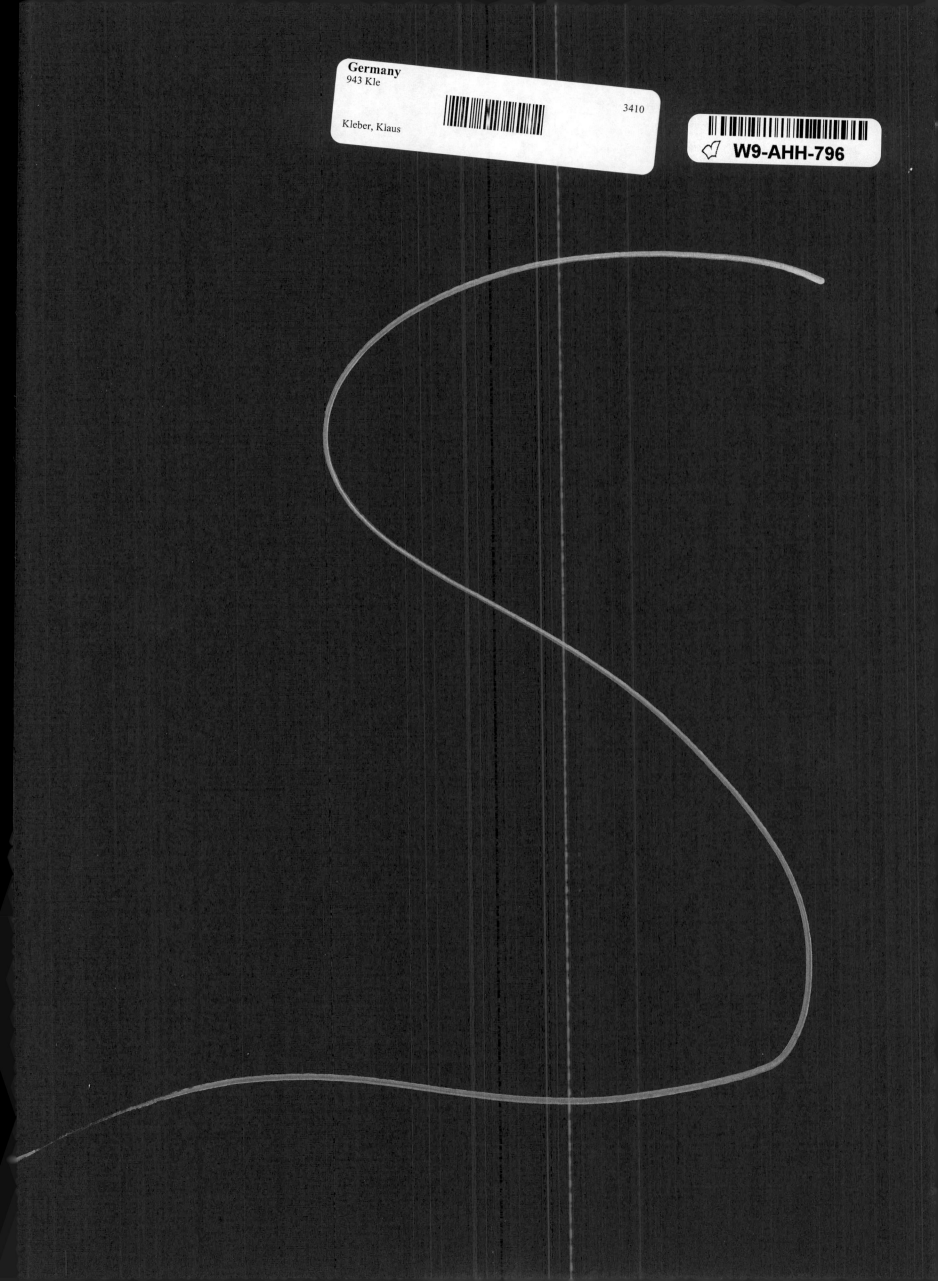

GERMANY

donated by Robert Garrison

GERMANY

PHOTOGRAPHY BY BRYAN F. PETERSON
TEXT BY KLAUS KLEBER

GRAPHIC ARTS CENTER PUBLISHING COMPANY
PORTLAND, OREGON

International Standard Book Number 1-55868-046-2
Library of Congress Number 91-71225
© MCMXCI by Graphic Arts Center Publishing Company
P.O. Box 10306 • Portland, OR 97210
All rights reserved. No part of this book
can be reproduced by any means
without written permission of the publisher.
President • Charles M. Hopkins
Editor-in-Chief • Douglas A. Pfeiffer
Managing Editor • Jean Andrews
Designer • Robert Reynolds
Cartographer • Manoa Mapworks, Inc.
Typographer • Harrison Typesetting, Inc.
Color Separations • Wy'East Color, Inc.
Printer • Rono Graphic Communications Co.
Bindery • Lincoln & Allen
Printed in the United States of America

Morning sun reflects in windows of Meissen's Gothic cathedral dating back to A.D. 929. Located in what was East Germany, Meissen is known for its porcelain, produced by Royal Porcelain Manufacture founded in 1710. ◄ ◄ ◄ The twin spires of Cologne's cathedral dwarf the statue of a horse and rider. ◄ ◄ The legendary Castle Neuschwanstein, commissioned by King Ludwig II of Bavaria, overlooks an Alpine countryside. ◄

GERMANY

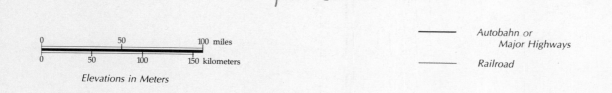

Flensburg, Germany's northernmost large town

A dream come true for a father, his son, his family, his friends—an entire nation. Stepping beyond the wall into freedom and learning to experience a new way of life— a breath of fresh air, quiet prayers answered. Along with them, 17.5 million former East Germans can finally do the same. ▲ During a dramatic sunset in what was East Germany, a young couple looks west. As the sun reflects in their eyes, their hearts are touched with a spark of freedom and the hope for a bright future as new members of a democratic free world that holds new promise for them. ▶

Patiently waiting for its *Frauchen* or *Herrchen* to come home, a cat stands guard at a century-old farmhouse entry. The strongly crafted, solid wood door features a wrought-iron *Briefschlitz,* or mailslot. The cobblestone street in front adds a rustic atmosphere. ◄ Pigeons abound in Germany, drinking from the thousands of fountains adorning marketplaces. *This* pigeon gets its water crystal-clear right from the source. ▲

Modern sculpture and present-day architecture mingle with remains of the past. Berlin, Germany's new capital, is known for its avant-garde art and sculpture in its streets and parks and in its hundreds of galleries and museums. ▲ Neckarstein, at the river Neckar, is famous for its four castles which overlook the township they protected throughout the Middle Ages. Each year in May, the dramatic Four Castles Illumination sparks fireworks above this twelfth-century town. Today, sections of the castles are baronial residences of a German aristocratic family. ▶

Germany, to me, was never West or East, we or they. It was always one—one in heart and spirit, one in history. Though it might have to wait for some distant future, it was destined to be one again.

Then, suddenly, that distant future became now, and what belonged together came together in a jubilant and peaceful expression of the German people's innermost desire for freedom and unity.

It defies description how I, along with millions of others, felt at that moment. An almost unbelievable series of events climaxed in the opening of the Wall and barbed-wire fences across Berlin and Germany, allowing hands to touch, forgotten smiles to be seen, and tears of joy to run freely.

Church bells rang across the country, from villages to cities, from hillsides to valleys, proclaiming a free people in a free and united country.

Today, the sounds and sights of *all* Germany welcome visitors from all over the world.

This book is an invitation to discover a country and a people that have so much to offer—to see the diversity of a nation rich in history and culture, reborn anew, and to experience the coming alive of history, the romance of an exciting countryside, and the hospitality of a great people.

Welcome to Germany!

One Germany!

Conversation with people I meet invariably includes the question, "Where are you from—I mean, originally?" (I guess twenty-five years in the United States have not erased my accent.)

"From Germany," I answer. They ask where in Germany, and I say, "Berlin."

"East or West?" they ask.

"West, but inside the East. . ." I say. They stare. "Well, let me explain. . ."

Conversations like this are a lot easier today, because the political geography of Germany is easier to explain. There is, finally, only one Germany and only one Berlin.

For almost half a century, Germany was divided. After World War II, it became the Federal Republic of Germany (West Germany) and the German Democratic Republic (East Germany), referred to as "the Russian Zone." West Germany included British (north), French (west) and American (south) occupation zones.

Berlin, an island city right in the center of East Germany, clearly reflected the country's division. East Berlin was the capital of East Germany, whereas the western part had a special Allied status and was part of the West.

When Germany became one again in 1990, and politics no longer interfered with geography, the location of my birthplace became much easier to explain. To describe the diverse landscape and scenery of my homeland, however, remains a challenge.

What I'd most like to say is, "Just go there and see for yourself."

"Go exactly where?" you say. Good question. Let me try to paint a picture so you can choose for yourself.

Germany is situated right in the heart of Europe, surrounded by more countries than any other European state. Germany touches Denmark to the north; Holland, Belgium, Luxembourg, and France to the west; Austria and Switzerland to the south; and Poland and Czechoslovakia to the east. To the west, east, and north, Germany has no natural borders. As a result, it has been for centuries a region of migration, allowing a free exchange of people, cultures, and ideas, which has left an impact on the character of Germany today.

Some twenty thousand years ago, the forces of melting ice carved out the land Germans call home and created the diversity of beautiful landscapes that welcome visitors to Germany today. From the seas to the mountains, from the forests to the rivers and lakes, bouquets of scenery unfold that keep travelers entranced.

West Germany divides naturally into three distinct geographic areas—the north German plains (or lowlands), the central German uplands and the Alpine foothills and Alps.

The broad horizons of the northern plains offer contrasts between lakes, canals and stretches of hills, between heaths and marshes, sandy downs and fens. These lowlands slope toward the sea. The North Sea coastline is devoid of cliffs and markedly different from the Baltic Sea coast, which is indented by small fjords with steep banks rising abruptly to beautiful, wooded slopes.

As you travel south into the central German uplands, the scenes change to hills, rich forest, and small mountain ranges, such as the Harz Peaks. In the scenic beauty of the Weserbergland, Teutoburger Wald, Sauerland, Bergisches Land and the Hessiches Bergland are hundreds of picturesque villages nestled among the hills. This particular region has inspired stories, legends, and fairy tales that have become part of the fantasies of thousands of children around the world.

Farther south, forest-rich hillsides frame colorful, wide, fertile valleys and romantic river gorges. The Rhine and Weser valleys, winding through Germany from south to north, are complemented

---

Coots at the shore of Lake Constance enjoy a leisurely evening swim. Lake Constance, located 1,295 feet high on the border of Switzerland and Austria, is the largest of the Alpine lakes. ◄

by the beauty of the Rivers Main and Danube, which divide the landscape west to east. Within this network of winding rivers, large and small, the mosaic pattern of the central upland hills creates an amazing variety of individual landscapes.

The River Rhine and its surroundings are, to many visitors, the essence of Germany. From its original spring in Switzerland, the Rhine flows through many beautiful areas, including the Black Forest, the wine region of Mainz, Wiesbaden and Bingen. At Koblenz, it connects with the River Mosel, bordering another valley famous for fine wines, then moves on to Cologne, and finally to the industrial area of the Ruhr Valley.

Although they are in the same geographic region, the Hunsrück and the Taunus have very different scenic personalities than the Spessart or the Swabian and Franconian *Albs,* the low hills adjoining the Alpine foothills. When travelers reach the famous Black Forest in the southwest corner of Germany, they will have collected impressions of nature's beauty and diversity that are unsurpassed in any other European country.

The once-blue Danube, made famous by composer Johann Strauss, marks the entrance into Germany's Alpine foothills. Crossing the Danube *(Donau)* into the gentle foothills of the Alps is like stepping through the door of yet another nature spectacular. Lush green pastures, hills, rock formations, wild rivers, and clear, quiet, wonderful lakes lead up to the majestic peaks of the Alps themselves. The German portions of the Alps include the Allgäuer Alps, the Bavarian Alps, and—to the east—the Salzburger Alps, all small in area but rich in variety of scenery.

Picturesque lakes nestle amidst the rugged Alps. Especially memorable is the Königssee and its steep and inaccessible banks, where the Chapel of St. Bartholomä seems to float on an island. I remember thinking, as I stood in this sanctuary setting as a young boy, that there could not be many more places in this world more beautiful, serene, and enchanting.

Lake Constance, Germany's largest natural lake, shares its shores with Germany, Austria, and Switzerland, and the majestic Swiss and Austrian Alps form a backdrop. The lake is more than eight hundred feet deep and seven miles wide. Set in this calm beauty is the picturesque island of Mainau, where an exceptionally mild climate supports one of the most beautiful botanical and tropical gardens in all of Europe.

The central section of the Bavarian Alps is a favorite among nature enthusiasts. From Garmisch-Partenkirchen, one can look up to the majestic and breathtaking splendor of Zugspitze, Germany's highest Alpine peak, at more than ninety-seven hundred feet.

Through it all winds the famous German Alpine Road, connecting Lake Constance in the west with Berchtesgaden, a wonderful ski resort, in the east. Between are sights and sounds so great and bountiful that, in one journey, it becomes difficult to take them all in. Every turn on the Alpine Road offers something new and spectacular.

Travelers are always pleased to discover that roads are good and well maintained in Germany. If you find it difficult, as I do, to orient yourself in *any* country according to topography, mountain ranges, and plateaus, consider this way of getting to know Germany: procure a car at the airport and just set out. On the all-covering network of Germany's famous Autobahn, you can experience true German *Fahrvergnügen,* the pleasure of driving. Or see the country on the extensive—and efficient—railroad system. Some general bearings are all you need. Remember that Hamburg is in the north, Munich is in the south, Cologne is in the west, Dresden is in the east, Frankfurt in the southwest, and Berlin in the northeast.

Or you can travel extensively by boat on the vast network of rivers. The Rhine, Weser, and Elbe flow almost parallel from southeast to northwest, with the Rhine on the west, the Weser in the center, the Elbe to the east; the river Oder forms the border with Poland. Traveling north from Munich, you'll cross the Danube, then the River Main and, in the north, the Überland Kanal, which cuts across northern Germany.

To get to know Germany is not only to enjoy its geography but also to get acquainted with its *Länder,* which are states like those in the United States. Including the newly formed East German states, there are now sixteen German *Länder,* three of which are city-states.

Bavaria (Bayern), the largest of the German states, is rich in lakes and forests. Bordered in the south by the beauty of perpetual snow and ancient glaciers in the rugged Alps, it extends north beyond the Danube to the river Main. Its capital, Munich, lying in the midst of the Alpine foothills, has been called "Germany's secret capital." It is home to BMW and the *Oktoberfest,* and was the site of the 1972 Summer Olympics.

Also located in Bavaria are the famous Castle Neuschwanstein; the Richard Wagner town of Bayreuth, known for its festivals; and the site of the world-famous passion plays, *Oberammergau.* Hundreds of quaint villages dot the quiet Bavarian countryside.

West of Bavaria, in the state of Baden-Württemberg, is the legendary Black Forest, dense with greenish-black trees. Long famous for beautiful, handcrafted cuckoo clocks, Baden-Württemberg is

now the most industrialized of the German *Länder*. Called the "high-tech" state, it is the headquarters of world-renowned companies such as Daimler-Benz, Porsche, and Bosch. Stuttgart is its capital. Heidelberg is the site of Germany's oldest university, made famous through the *Studentenprinz* and festivals of song and beer.

In Rhineland-Palatine (Rheinland-Pfalz), to the northwest across the River Rhine, is Germany's main wine-producing region. Two-thirds of German vineyards are along the Rivers Mosel, Ahr, and Rhine. Its many castle ruins, volcanic lakes, and old Roman towers create some of Germany's most beautiful landscapes.

The smallest of the German *Länder*, not including the three city-states, is the Saarland, to the southwest of Rhineland-Palatine. Bordering France and Luxembourg, it is known for its coal and steel industries. The gentle, wooded slopes of the Saar Valley are dotted with orchards, vineyards, and idyllic villages.

In Hesse lies the almost two-thousand-year-old metropolis of Frankfurt, Germany's financial capital. Also called the "gateway to the world" because of its busy international airport, Frankfurt is the center of one of Germany's major economic regions.

Along with Thüringen to the east, Hesse forms the heart of Germany and the link between North and South. Known for its many elegant health spas, it also contains the thick mountain ranges of the Vogelsberg, Taunus, Spessart and Odenwald, almost untouched by civilization.

The most populous state in Germany is North-Rhine Westphalia (Nordrhein-Westfalen) in the northwest. From there, Charlemagne ruled Europe's largest empire between A.D. 768 and 843. Known for the industrial Ruhr region, with its mining, steel, and iron industries, North-Rhine Westphalia is also rich in agriculture and diversified industry, including some of Germany's largest breweries.

Europe's largest inland port, Duisburg, is located in North-Rhine Westphalia. The state's lively economy is reflected in a densely knit network of transportation facilities. Bonn, Beethoven's town, was Germany's capital from 1949 to 1990. Since Germany's unification, Berlin has once again become the capital, but most administrative government activities still take place in Bonn. The Münsterland, in the northern part of North-Rhine Westphalia, is well known for its flat, parklike scenery, majestic farms, water palaces and romantic chapels and churches.

Lower Saxony (Niedersachen), the second largest German state, extends in the northwest from the North Sea coast to the central German uplands. It includes the Weserbergland and the Harz Mountains, with their unique rock formations, and more than seventy lakes and ponds. North of Hannover, the state's capital, is

Germany's oldest nature preserve, Luneberg Heath (Lüneburger Heide)—peaceful acres of juniper shrubs, pine trees, and flocks of sheep. In the fall, the area lights up with the glow of purple heather.

Lower Saxony is also a major agricultural region, second only to Bavaria, and it is of special economic importance because of its natural gas and petroleum reserves in the north. The internationally successful Volkswagen company is in Wolfburg.

The East Frisian Islands, the Steinhuder Meer (a thirty-square-mile inland lake), and the area around Hameln are favorite tourist sights. The land around Hameln, along the river Weser, is rich with stories, from Medieval sagas to Grimm's fairy tales.

Within Lower Saxony is the smallest of the German states, the city-state known as the Free and Hanseatic City of Bremen, which consists of the cities of Bremen and Bremerhaven. It was founded in the eighth century and became, along with Hamburg and Lübeck, one of the leading members of the Hanseatic League, dominating trade in the North and Baltic Sea regions. Important for shipbuilding and fishing, Bremen is Germany's second most important port and one of the world's leading seaports.

The second German city-state, the Free and Hanseatic City of Hamburg, is located between Lower Saxony and Schleswig-Holstein. Situated at the northern tip of the river Elbe, where it enters the North Sea, Hamburg is Germany's largest, most important seaport. Founded in the ninth century, Hamburg, like Bremen, has maintained a special independent city-state status because of its centuries-old influence and power in world trade.

The northernmost German state is Schleswig-Holstein. The only state that borders on both the North Sea and the Baltic Sea, it has Denmark as its northern neighbor. It is predominantly agricultural and is well known for producing fine cattle and pigs. Attractions include the red rock isle of Helgoland, rising steeply from the North Sea; the old Hanseatic city of Lübeck, with its impressive, patrician homes; and Holstein's Switzerland (Holsteiner Schweiz), with dozens of mirrorlike, solitary lakes lying amidst thick forests. Beautiful and distinctly different beaches on both seas, with colorful vistas of skies and sand, make Schleswig-Holstein a summer vacation paradise.

Actually, most of Germany is a vacation paradise. As a child, I often wondered why we went to Italy, Switzerland, or Austria instead of exploring more of our own country. I guess getting out of Berlin and Germany and discovering the cultures of our neighbors seemed more important after the years of the war.

Now that I live in the United States and visit annually, I probably have seen more of Germany's sights I *wanted* to see than when I

actually lived there. And because I look at Germany more as a visitor now, I gain perspective and insights I never had before. That is especially true when I return to Berlin, also a city-state and the "new" German capital.

Located in the heart of the state of Brandenburg, Berlin is a city full of scenic beauty, of rivers, lakes, forest, hills and beaches—almost a country to itself. Berlin is my hometown, my birthplace, and home to family and friends with whom I have shared many special moments in my life. It also has a special place in my heart as a city that belongs not only to Germany, but to the world, to the people of America and the rest of the global community. Therefore, it will have a special place in this book, and I will come back to it as we continue to travel through Germany together.

When I explored Germany with my parents as a boy, and later by myself and with my own family, our travels were always limited to the West, except for what we saw on both sides of the Autobahn when traveling through the Russian Zone to and from Berlin. Then we saw the sad faces of East Germans, young and old, who waved at us from overpasses as we traveled between points of freedom.

Recalling the expressions on those faces, I am reminded of a line of German poetry, *Die Gedanken sind frei, wer kann sie erraten,* "The thoughts are free—who can guess them." It seems to symbolize the perseverance and inner strength of East Germans, who endured a repressive political system for so many decades.

During the years of occupation, the East was sealed off. Right through the heart of Germany and Berlin, over fourteen hundred kilometers of barbed wire stretched north to south, watched closely by border guards with orders to shoot to kill. When my family traveled, many of the beautiful roads we took ended in roadblocks, border signs, and guard stations. We wondered what it would be like to be able to travel and see the "other" Germany.

In 1990, my "wondering thoughts" became a heart-moving and emotional reality. For the first time in my life, I could travel freely through East Germany and East Berlin without having to stop anywhere. What an indescribable, joyful feeling it was!

The people of East Germany rejoiced even more in the reunion with the West. Demonstrating their commitment to the restoration of their cultural and historical past, they discarded the centralized communist government structure and revived the pre-communist *Länder* divisions.

With the unification of Germany and the election of an all-German parliament, the German Federal Republic welcomed five new *Länder.* Reborn in the east are Brandenburg, Sachsen-Anhalt, Sachsen, Mecklenburg-Vorpommern, and Thüringen.

Reunion with West Germany has also resulted in a resurfacing of East German culture, history, and a true identity of its own. During the past few decades, the Western world tended to attribute many notable cultural and historical events and people of the past to "West Germany" when, in actuality, they took place in, and belonged to, the East. So East Germany brings with it not only a beautiful landscape, but also a rich and abundant cultural history, only vaguely recognized until the political borders between East and West Germany opened and vanished.

The natural geographic sections of East Germany are the Baltic coastline, the Northern Lowlands, and the Southern Uplands, a region of hills, mountains, and woodlands.

In the north, the landscape of Brandenburg is a mix of marsh, sand, and pine woods, laced with rivers and dotted with lakes. The famous Spreewald, with its network of streams and rivers, once drew many Berliners on outings, with picnic baskets in their boats. Poland borders Brandenburg to the east, across the River Oder.

The heart of the Kingdom of Prussia during the eighteenth century, when Frederick the Great reigned over the German states, Brandenburg is especially rich in culture and history.

Near Potsdam, the capital of Brandenburg, lies the famous Sans Souci Palace which was built by Frederick the Great. Painters von Menzel and Liebermann, philosophers Hegel and Spranger, scientists Alexander and Wilhelm von Humboldt, poet von Kleist, and architects Schinkel and Shadow all lived and worked in the city of Potsdam.

North of Brandenburg is the state of Mecklenburg-Vorpommern, famous for its healthy climate. It is also called "the land of a thousand lakes and castles." Heinrich Schliemann, the discoverer of Troy; composer Frederick von Flotow; and sculptor Ernst Barlach all called the Baltic Sea state their home.

In Mecklenburg-Vorpommern are renowned shipyards and the beautiful seaside resorts of the Baltic Sea. Resorts stretch from the Bay of Lübeck to the isle of Rügen, Germany's largest island, then on to Kühlungsborn and the spa of Ahlbeck. The people of Mecklenburg-Vorpommern have great hope that the once-famous spas and other resorts will be renovated to again attract visitors from all over the world.

It was in Kühlungsborn that the famous *Strandkorb* was created. This wicker beach chair for two, with its adjustable top and colorful canvas awning, now dots every European beach.

Like Brandenburg, Mecklenburg-Vorpommern borders Poland to the east. Saxony, to its south, shares a common border with Poland and Czechoslovakia.

Saxony is the most industrialized of the East German *Länder*. During the final days of the war in 1945, Saxony's capital, Dresden, was reduced to rubble in an Allied bomb attack, and tens of thousands lost their lives. Since then, some of the destroyed cultural landmarks have been restored to their former splendor. A capital-funds campaign is under way to finance the rebuilding of the famous Frauenkirche, the finest baroque structure in East Germany. The city of Meissen, where the world-famous porcelain factory of the same name is located, is also in Saxony.

Saxony's contributions to world culture include the work of composers Carl Maria von Weber, Richard Wagner, and Richard Strauss; philosophers Leibniz and Frichte; arithmetician Adam Riese; and writers Joachim Ringelnatz and Erich Kästner.

The state of Sachsen-Anhalt, the center of the chemical industry in East Germany, stretches across the plains on both sides of the Rivers Saale and Elbe. It was in the city of Torgan, in southeastern Saxony-Anhalt on the River Elbe, that the Soviet Army and the Allied troops met in 1945 to seal Hitler's defeat. Today, Sachsen-Anhalt presents the greatest environmental clean-up challenge in Germany. Polluted water, soil, and air pose much danger to residents.

Composer Georg Friedrich Händel came from Saxony-Anhalt, as did foreign minister Hans-Dietrich Genscher, who played a major international role in the unification process.

Because Thüringen, the fifth of the East German *Länder*, boasts so much woodland between the Thüringen Forest and the Harz mountains, it is known as the "green heart of Germany." It is also famous for its engineering plants and glassworks, and for the Carl Zeiss optical instrument works in Jena.

Thüringen has been the birthplace of many major political events and movements, including Martin Luther's Reformation and the Peasant War of the sixteenth century. It was in the Wartburg, a castle near Eisenach, that Luther began to translate the Bible into German, and there, in 1817, students assembled to call for German unity.

It was in the cities of Gotha and Erfurt that the German Social Democratic Party was formed in the late 1800s, and in Weimar that the Constituent Assembly of the first German Republic convened in 1919 to create the Weimar Republic. Goethe and Schiller lived in Weimar, the city that nurtured German classicism. Johann Sebastian Bach was born in Eisenach and, between 1723 and 1750, composed in Leipzig.

Now that Germany is again one, each of the five East German *Länder* will play a major role in reforging German economic, philosophic, and psychological unity. Each returns special treasures to the table of a united Germany.

Germany's grid of rivers and streams, dotted with lakes and ponds and topped by hills and mountains, is a geography so rich in beauty it inevitably inspires song and poetry. In geography class, my grade-school teacher intertwined German music with her favorite subject. We heard musical praise of our land, *Von den Alpen bis zur Waterkant*, "From the Alps to the Edge of the Sea." We sang of the "heather's sun glow," the "shining of the stars," the "song of the birds," the "wind in the woods," and "God's Beautiful Land" with its *Bächleiu, Wald, and Felder*, "Streams, Forests, and Fields."

Now, once again, all of the 78.5 million Germans, across all of Germany's nearly 140,000 square miles, are learning Germany's whole geography, traveling without borders and singing old songs and new, together. Germany's rich heritage and culture once more belong equally to everyone.

The German nation grew out of a large number of individual tribes, including the Franks, the Frisians, and the Saxons, the Thüringians, the Bavarians, the Swabians, and the Alemanians. These tribal divisions are still recognizable today in the German *Bundesländer*, which now compose the Federal Republic.

Germany's quest for democratic nationhood spans more than a thousand years. It was in the eighth century, under Charlemagne, that people speaking German and Romance dialects joined, and the word *Deutsch* (German) began to be used. Under the Treaty of Verdun, created in A.D. 843, Charlemagne's grandsons divided his extensive empire into eastern and western sections, from which Germany and France developed. What followed was what one of my history teachers once called a "roller coaster" of divisions, additions, disintegrations, power build-ups, competition, and intrigue. Germany emerged as a people struggling to find a common denominator and a sense of belonging.

The sixteenth century brought to Germany Luther's Reformation and a division of the church. The Counter Reformation followed, leading to the Thirty Years' War and Germany's devastation by other European powers. In 1648, after the Treaty of Westphalia, two German powers established themselves, Prussia and Hapsburg-Austria. Prussia became a power of great stature under Frederick the Great.

At the end of the eighteenth century, Napoleon I created a west, central, and south Germany under his power. With the collapse of Napoleon's empire in 1806, national uprisings and wars for liberation climaxed in the Congress of Vienna, which established thirty-nine German sovereign states and cities.

In 1834, the Prussian leadership formed the German Customs Union and provided economic unity. This was followed, after the 1848 March Revolution, by Germany's first democratically elected National Assembly. Separation from Austria and establishment of the North German Federation came after the German War of 1866.

After the Franco-German War of 1870 and as a result of the Treaty of Versailles in 1871, the Second German Reich, under Emperor Wilhelm I of Prussia, emerged. Political parties then expanded their influence. The end of World War I in 1918 marked the end of the dynasties that had ruled Germany for so long and had led into the founding of the Weimar Republic.

The darkest period of recent German history began when, under Adolf Hitler, the National Socialism Party came to power in 1933. Hitler's inhumane, reckless, and deceitful leadership led to World War II in 1939 and ended in 1945 with the total collapse and division of the German Third Reich. The result was the formation of the German Democratic Republic under communist rule in the East and the Federal Republic of Germany in the West.

West Germany's first president, Theodor Heuss, and its first chancellor, Konrad Adenauer, became the champions of a new democratic Germany, leading its citizens, amidst a new-found freedom of expression and political liberty, towards a new constitution with liberty and justice for all. Thus the country and its people emerged to become partners, instead of adversaries, in an international, global community of nations.

Discussing Germany's historic past, its recent past under the Third Reich, and the country as it is today, a friend and I concluded that countries, like people—like the two of us—derive their "personalities" from the circumstances under which they "grew up." Their behavior is the culmination of all that is, and was in their past, and they, too, have the ability to learn and to change. They can, despite "molestations in the past," be new "people" with new beginnings.

Recognizing its past and choosing a new future, Germany has become a new "person"—strongly differentiating the good from the evil without losing awareness of its rich and abundant history and heritage.

This new thinking, we concluded, lets us be proud of who we are and where we came from, because we know where Germany is going.

Much has been said about the German personality—some of it not quite right. I remember distinctly when I first came to the United States and saw the television show, "Hogan's Heroes." Was this how Americans saw the Germans? I wavered between being shocked and insulted, concluding that it is no wonder that nations don't get along when the media distort reality. However, since then, I learned to laugh at the Germans and at myself. I also learned about the American culture and its ability to poke fun and take things more lightly.

In that sense, Germans have become more "Americanized" today. Still, to Americans, Germans often appear formal and reserved. That is definitely part of the German culture, but it is also true that today's young Germans tend to be more informal and accepting, due, in part, to extensive travel by German business people and tourists, to youth exchanges, and to a definite movement toward "Europeanization" and "internationalization."

At times, Germans seem to be people of contradiction. They can be very romantic, playful, informal, artistic, yet they also can appear to be very reserved, exact, precise, industrious—keeping most of who they are to themselves. They can, on occasion, be very opinionated and inflexible, yet they can also be most accommodating and open-minded.

Germans are also considered to be very thorough with respect to detail. Now that I travel through Germany as a German-American, I find my own Germanic traits confirmed many times over. When I ask for directions to a certain place, I always get more—including the history of the site, where I can get more information, and when it is the best time to visit. And often someone says, "Come with me, I'll show you."

Today's German is very European but has a strong sense of national pride. The fact that this pride does not appear openly has its reasons, in part, in Germany's recent past.

In addition to a commitment to the united Europe and a global society, Germans have a strong and unwavering commitment to insuring that the recent past does not repeat itself. Their hands are stretched to others across their borders in a gesture of reconciliation, reaching for a lasting peace, understanding, and friendship that knows no boundaries of any sort.

There is hardly a place in Germany that does not remind its people, young and old, of the horrors of that short, but cruel, decade in its long and rich history of contributions to the world. Monuments and signs, places and people—all tell Germans never to forget, but to learn and to move on with consideration, sensitivity, and new vision.

The German people of today, in more than one way, have come out of their shell. No longer willing to almost blindly "follow their leader," a tendency acquired through hundreds of years of

conditioning by the kings, princes, bishops, and other figures of authority, they are also striving to be themselves and not what they think others might expect of them.

However, Germans still like things to be "just right," and, if possible, perfect. They are driven by a devotion to thoroughness in things small or large and still retain a commitment to their traditional customs and values.

Germans are also guided by the customs and culture of their own regions. Even though certain general German personality traits can be attributed to all, different nuances can be found in each state. People have kept their own dialects and their very own traditions and customs, including the way they dress and celebrate festivities.

Traveling across the country and observing Germans, you will find that people in the north, in cities like Hamburg, are quite a bit more formal and reserved than people in the south. In Munich, everyone acts more outgoing, jovial, and festive. Where a handshake welcomes you in Berlin, it is not uncommon to see people in Munich hugging and greeting one another with, *"Grüss Gott"* (God bless you) in contrast to the *"Guten Tag"* (Good day) elsewhere.

In other words, Germans are as diverse a people as their country is in its landscape. They are artists, writers, musicians, engineers, educators—all people who want to enjoy life to the fullest, who are creative and resourceful and who, because of their country's past, have become individually and collectively an international people, perhaps more so than any other country in the world. This international spirit is expressed in that Germans enjoy travel, adventure, and far-away, exotic places—including the Far East, the South Pacific, Texas, California, New York, and Oregon (which I call "my other Germany").

Germans have always been fascinated with America and with Americans. They admire the easygoing lifestyle and the American ingenuity, and they have developed, during the past decades, a certain degree of kinship with their friends across the Atlantic. I remember my fascination with America as a young boy, chewing American gum, admiring American cars parked in the streets by GIs, seeing Western movies, and playing the old game of "Cowboys and Indians." in the streets of my neighborhood. Perhaps it was then, when Germans admired all things "Made in America," that I set my sights on someday seeing this great place far away.

In addition to diversity of landscapes and people, Germany also displays a rich cultural diversity.

Well into the nineteenth century, Germany was divided among a great number of potentates. Each sovereignty, large or small, had its own cultural center, with its own theater, concert hall, university, and art collection. Competition among these sovereignties resulted in the multitude of cultural centers Germany enjoys today.

The outcome of this emphasis on cultural autonomy, added to the regionalism of the various German states, is that Germany has never developed a predominant cultural metropolis, as neighboring countries have. Germany's many distinct centers make cultural activities easily accessible and cultural life especially rich.

Another result of nineteenth-century regionalism and competition is specialization. There are more theaters in Munich, but more art galleries and museums in Berlin. The central library of Germany is in Frankfurt, but the largest archives are in the small town of Marbach. However, one need not travel far in Germany to hear a good concert or see a great play. Cultural centers can be found in every city, and many of the medium-sized German towns maintain valuable libraries and rich art collections. Today, Germany has more than five hundred theaters and opera houses, well over a hundred major orchestras, and more than two thousand museums of different kinds. In this way, Germans now reap the benefits of earlier rulers' regional ambitions.

Germans also value the printed word. That Germans love to read is evident in the large selection of magazines, dailies, and weeklies and the abundance of literary and technical works in ever-present bookstores all over Germany. Being well-read is a source of status in German society; and reading, a true German pastime. Whenever I visited my grandfather in East Berlin, he read to me. Sometimes it would be just the *Brockhaus,* the German equivalent of Webster's Dictionary, which he knew from cover to cover. He would say, "Read whenever you can, wherever you can, whatever you can so you'll be a learned person and become successful in life."

Culture in Germany manifests itself not only in the beauty of the well-kept countryside but also in the baroque architecture and art and the almost countless castles. But its ultimate evidence is in the spiritual expressions of a people and their respect and honor for an ever-present, almighty God. German cathedrals, as symbols of that respect, are the culmination of medieval architecture. Entire generations of designers, architects, and laborers worked on them without ever seeing the completed results of their labors.

More than forty such cathedrals still stand, some destroyed and rebuilt, in major cities throughout Germany. They reflect not only determination and highly skilled workmanship, but the special civic spirit that prevailed in medieval times and an outspoken respect for God, symbolized in the crosses that crown almost every cathedral tower.

Churches and cathedrals in Germany have always inspired me and left me in awe, feeling respect and admiration, not only for those whose lives built them but also what they represent. In a Gothic cathedral, a person experiences a oneness with God in a special way, feeling surrounded by the heavens; time stands still, and voices of the past, present, and future are all with you at once.

Germans show a great respect for religion, the symbols of its establishment and its meaning in their daily lives. Like the cathedrals in their majestic, yet quiet, presence, Germans keep their beliefs mostly to themselves. You have to get really close to experience them, too.

As scenic beauty and history are an integral part of the German fiber, so is art. Interested or not, one is constantly confronted with it, not only in museums, but even in the streets. Historians consider the birthplace of German art to be in Aachen, in the palace chapel of Charlemagne, dating from the year A.D. 800.

After the Middle Ages and the flowering of the Renaissance, Germany came into its own during the rich and productive period titled "baroque." Between A.D. 1600-1750, this original style influenced the creation of literature, art, and music.

The culmination of German baroque music was in the works of Johann Sebastian Bach and George Friedrich Händel. Concerts of baroque music are held year after year in handsome baroque buildings throughout southern Germany, as well as Berlin and Dresden. Architectural examples of "flowering baroque" can be found in nearly all southern German cities. Journeys into the baroque, late baroque, and rococo can start at Stuttgart via Tübingen, Sigmaringen, Lindau, and on to Ulm.

Baroque style gave way to rococo, followed by the classical period ending in 1850. The classical revival, in the second half of the nineteenth century, was succeeded by a pluralism of styles, including Neo-Gothic and Neo-classical, as well as the *Jugendstil* of the 1890s, and—later—the expressionists. Today's architectural style is still influenced by the famous Bauhaus School of Walter Gropius, a functional, experimental architecture utilizing all the resources of art, science, and technology.

Today, in German architecture and art, examples of all these styles coexist in apparent harmony. The old and historic mixes everywhere with the modern and futuristic—without creating a dissonance. Germany has, during the post-war years, encouraged the best of modern and functional architecture and easily can be seen as a global trendsetter.

Germans are constantly surrounded by music. The first German hymn was written by Luther and Walther in the early sixteenth century. The first German opera, *Daphne,* was composed in 1627, and the first German opera house opened in Hamburg in 1678. Bach's and Handel's passions, oratorios, organ music, and cantatas still bring delight to music lovers all over the world, and the works of Haydn, Mozart, and Beethoven are listened to more than modern rock. The movement toward realism in music was led by Wagner, followed by the great symphonists of the nineteenth century, Bruckner, Brahms, and Mahler.

Martin Luther's translations of the Bible led to a high German literary language, and printing made possible a wider readership. Popular books were *Eulenspiegel* and *Faust.*

Permanent theaters were erected in the middle of the seventeenth century. Major forces in the formation of the German theater were the dramas and dramaturgy of Lessing. Goethe and Schiller brought about the transition to classicism and, together with Kleist and Hoelderlin, became the literary standard which continued into the twentieth century.

Critical realism was introduced by Heine, Buchner, and Fontane. Naturalism came with Mann, Hauptmann, and Wedekind. Kraus, Tucholsky, and especially Brecht set standards in Germany for a social realism, not only describing, but wanting to change, society. They became models for the current generation of authors, including Grass, Boell, Walser, Weiss, Handke, and others.

Germany has not only brought forth an impressive number of composers, writers, and artists throughout centuries, but through them it has also developed in its people a genuine love and admiration of artistic works.

One of the nice things about being in Germany is that one can still visit many places where famous people were born or lived. In Frankfurt, the house in which Goethe was born and grew up is open to visitors. In Bonn, one can spend time in the house where Beethoven was born. Another place of interest is the museum in Garmisch-Partenkirchen, which is devoted to Richard Strauss, of *der Rosenkavalier* fame. Nürnberg opens its Dürer house for visitors to discover how Albrecht Dürer once lived.

On another note, you can be one of the thousands of visitors annually at the Daimler-Benz museum in Stuttgart and discover how cars looked in 1885.

In Germany, almost every city has someone it is proud of—a composer, painter, poet, scientist, engineer, or philosopher. You can encounter them as monuments in the town square or in a museum built in their honor, with a comprehensive display of their work. In the small university town of Marburg on the Neckar, the National Museum honors Fredrick von Schiller. A museum in

Remscheid displays the work of its native son, Wilhelm Röntgen, who discovered X-ray. On the banks of the Neckar, in the romantic university town of Tübingen, stands the tower in which the poet Friedrich Hölderlin lived for many years. The invention of printing with movable type is explained in the museum of Mainz, where Johannes Gutenberg is honored.

German art can also be very personal, even political, expressing deep-down feelings of an era in both its beauty and its terror. Examples are the art created during the Third Reich and, on a different plane, the art not on paper or canvas but on the rough and inhuman surface of the Wall in Berlin, all twenty-five miles long. It was a museum of expressions of all sorts, in color, black and white, and in verse or political slogan. It was art by the people on one side and for the people on the other side. Ironically, the audience could not see this art of compassion and outcry until the Wall came down.

Living in Germany means living with art. Every room in my parents' home had paintings, mostly originals, wood carvings, statues, and other collectibles. There were no bare walls, and there are virtually no bare walls anywhere else in Germany.

My grandfather always told me, "If you can't read about another people, look at their art and it will help you understand them," and sometimes he would say, "Don't tell me, draw me a picture and color it," challenging early my creative abilities. Creativity, too, is high on the list of things you can observe and experience throughout all of Germany, crossing every fiber of life and region.

Education is an important and integral part of German society. Germany's educational system dates back to the founding of the country's first university in 1386. Attendance at German schools, from kindergarten through university, is free and paid for through the deutsche tax marks of its citizens. Compulsory education begins at the age of six and continues for nine to ten years, depending on the state. Students who opt for the *Gymnasium* attend for thirteen years to obtain *Abitur,* a diploma that qualifies them for admission to any of the 238 institutions of higher education.

One notable difference between German and American schools is that religious instruction is a regular subject in the German school system, demanded by German Basic Law. Many states have interdenominational schools oriented towards Christian principles.

The majority of young Germans begin their career preparation after completing nine or ten years of full-time schooling. They receive training in dual systems, in which on-the-job internships and instruction are combined with compulsory attendance at a part-time secondary or vocational school.

Germany's high industrialization and leadership in technological development and world trade can be attributed to its excellent education system, which produces highly skilled individuals in all levels of business and industry.

German integration of vocational training with the educational system dates back to the guilds of the Middle Ages. It has resulted in a labor force with standards second to none, plus the flexibility and foresight to use advanced production techniques. Costs are thereby reduced and quality enhanced, making the German economy more internationally competitive and successful.

Combine this with the innovation and creativity of the cultural arts, medicine, and other professional fields, and one can clearly see the virtues of a sound educational system and philosophy for any country, exemplified in the advances and progress of the German people.

When I saw a group of schoolchildren last summer, I was reminded of a German tradition that expresses how the German people feel about education and children. On my very first day in school, anxious and hesitant, I was comforted by my parents' presence and my *Schultute*—a large, beautifully decorated paper cone filled with chocolate, candy, and other small gifts. I remember it certainly made leaving the house and going to school a lot easier.

Education and learning are taken very seriously in Germany, and high-school life is much less social than it is in America. The only social activities I remember were a few school dances, plus formal dance and etiquette training at a nearby evening school. Attending such training means a young person has "come of age." Normally, students attend at about sixteen years old, right after *Konfirmation* (confirmation), which is still the custom for both Catholics and Evangelical Lutherans in Germany.

Because of the influence of German immigrants to the United States, Americans hold many things in common with Germans. One such import is the *Kindergarten,* the "children's garden," which, in Germany, supports and supplements the upbringing of three- to six-year-olds.

Well-educated teachers are the backbone of the German school system. Much is demanded of them, but they are paid well and enjoy the same respect and status as do other professionals such as lawyers and medical doctors.

Today, Germany is one of the leading industrial nations in the world; it is also one of the richest. Every fourth citizen of the European community comes from Germany. Germany ranks third in land area, after France and Spain.

Following two world wars that ended in such devastating defeats, Germany renewed her energy and grasped "the advantage of the defeated"—a phrase coined by Thomas Mann, the world-famous author. Mann's phrase captures the spirit of Germany, meaning that those who lose it all are more able to start anew. Receptive and open-minded, eager for action and change, today's Germans meet the challenges of the present with new ideas and find in them new opportunities.

Visiting Germany today, one can see the transformation and reconstruction, and sense the newness reflected in the lifestyles, technology, urban development, art, literature, and music. Most significant of all are the changes in industry and economy. There is yet another energy and thrust—economic, industrial, and materialistic, yet spiritual—pulling together fellow countrymen and women East and West, in a new focus on unity, on rebuilding and restoring, after a defeat of a different kind.

West Germany experienced the *Wirtschaftswunder,* or economic miracle. Now everyone is watching to see whether East Germany can follow suit and be rebuilt with the same success, in an even shorter period of time.

In 1945, no one dared to think that there would ever be another German state. In 1949, the picture already had changed, and, on May 23 of that year, the Federal Republic of Germany was proclaimed, followed by the creation of the Russian-occupied German Democratic Republic. Then, almost exactly four decades later, something else happened that no one dared to think. Peacefully, these two German parts became one again, united under the name of the Federal Republic of Germany.

Today, Germany has a solid foundation through its Basic Law, *Grundgesetz,* guaranteeing the rights of people in a free and democratic society—the equivalent to the American Constitution and Bill of Rights. It also was written into the Basic Law that "the entire German people are called upon to achieve in free self-determination the unity and freedom of Germany." In Germany, the legislative, executive, and judicial powers are exercised by separate divisions of the government that, as in the United States, constitute a system of checks and balances. As promised by the German Basic Law, the German people, too, have their rights for legal recourse against the misuse of government power.

In what I consider an unimaginably wonderful fulfillment of millions of constant, quiet prayers, Germany now has gained its rightful and completely recognized place in our family of nations.

People in Germany speak critically of the government and the malaise of bureaucracies, but in a different way than we do in America. Here we seem to have a distant, even adversarial view of *the* government rather than *our* government. In Germany, people appear to feel that they *are* the government, that their tax monies are spent where they should be, and, if not, they will see to it that they are. They also seem to "manage" government more like a business and get involved in fewer votes on issues. Germans are inclined to let those in power and position "do their job."

The most important legislative body is the German *Bundestag,* the House of Representatives, whose members are elected every four years in direct, free, and secret ballot elections by the German people. The majority of members of the *Bundestag* belong to the CDU/CSU, the SPD, the FDP or the Green Party.

The *Bundesrat,* or Federal Council, represents the German federal principle and provides participation of the individual states in federal, legislative, and executive government.

The chancellor and the federal ministers compose the federal cabinet of Germany. The federal president is the head of state who appoints the chancellor once he has been elected by the *Bundestag.*

The independence of the German states as part of the federation enables regional distinctions to be recognized and also gives opportunities for initiatives that, in a centralized state, would be impossible. At the same time, through its own *Länderparliaments* and *Ländergovernments,* it distributes power and makes sure that it is not abused by its central bodies—thus providing opportunity for distinction and local initiative.

Germans like to talk politics. As a matter of fact, I recently was talking with a school friend from Germany, who was vacationing and conducting some business in Florida. Right away, we got into the latest in politics: what party will join forces with what other party; the next election and how the former Communist Party in East Germany, now called PDS, strives to gain new influence; and how much disagreement there is over the relocation of certain government functions from Bonn, Germany's former capital, to Berlin, Germany's metropolis in the north and our hometown.

We also talked about Helmut Kohl, the German chancellor, who was at the right place at the right time and did the right thing. He seized the opportunity and, by doing it so forthrightly, displayed qualities of courage, great determination, and conviction not seen in him before. He will, we concluded, go down in history as a great political leader, on the same level as Konrad Adenauer. We felt that if he had not asserted his vision for a united Germany now, it might never have been realized. In the political climate that presents itself today, there probably would have evolved a more free, yet still communist and separate, other German country.

We could have talked all evening, but we were both busy, so I wished him a good flight (with Lufthansa, of course) and best wishes to his family and my Berlin. Right afterwards, I got a little bit of *Heimweh* (homesickness).

Heimweh nach dem Kurfürstendamm, "homesick for the Prince's Boulevard," is the title of just one of many songs about Berlin, a great city which is hard to forget, once you have been there.

Berlin was the capital of the German Reich between 1871 and 1945. Today, it is the capital of a united Germany. Like Hamburg and Bremen, Berlin is a city-state. It is Germany's largest industrial city and one of Europe's major conference and trade-fair cities. Founded in the thirteenth century, Berlin was by 1920 the third-largest city in the world. It is now home to 3.4 million Berliners.

The cultural wealth of the city is impressive. In addition to major art and ethnological museums and internationally renowned art galleries, Berliners have at their disposal over twenty theaters, two opera houses, several symphony orchestras, and a host of cabarets. Berlin's outstanding nightlife adds to the fact that Berlin is known as a city that is awake twenty-four hours a day.

Berliners are known for their dry sense of humor, their ability to poke fun at themselves and their sense of political survival, proved during the four trying decades leading up to the greatest party in the history of Berlin—the celebration of the opening of the Wall.

Protestant refugees arriving in 1685 in Berlin as a result of persecution under Louis XIV left a major impact on the city. These Huguenots influenced the architecture of Berlin and made major contributions to trade and industry, including the porcelain, textiles, scientific instruments, clocks, and musical instruments for which Berlin is also world famous. The fact that my family traces its history to the Huguenots gave me a real sense of belonging as I grew up in Berlin.

Of course, Berlin has a special place in my life and heart. Often, I feel as though I had never left it—*once a Berliner, always a Berliner.* Each time I visit and stay with my sister and her family or see my aunt and grandmother and friends, I add new memories, and old memories—good and bad—are revived. After the war, when there was very little to eat, Oma made tea out of apple peelings and "transferred" my pet rabbit from his cage to our table. I also remember as a little boy the sounds of American airplanes, sometimes as many as a thousand a day, that landed at the Berlin-Tempelhof Airport, bringing food to our city, because the Russians had set up a blockade. We called them *Rosinenbombers,* (raisin bombers) because they not only brought items that enabled the city to survive, but they also brought sweets for us kids, including raisins.

I remember standing on the other side of the *Potsdamerplatz* in 1953 watching helplessly the uprising of my fellow countrymen crushed by Russian tanks. Then in 1961, on August 13, I saw Germans on the other side of Berlin become instruments of terror, dividing my city in two by building what must have been the most inhumane wall in the world's history. Just the week before, I had seen my grandmother and my aunts at our house for *Kaffee und Kuchen* (afternoon coffee). Because they lived in East Berlin, it was years before I could see them again, and then only at their house. They were not allowed to come to ours.

I remember standing in front of the city hall of Berlin and hearing President Kennedy say, *"Ich bin ein Berliner"* (I am a Berliner). It was a moving and proud experience that is with me to this day. It symbolized not only history in the making and the heightening of the Cold War conflict, but also the strength of friendship. Without the Americans' help after the war, through the air blockade and building of the Wall, the city of Berlin and its people could not have survived. His visit emphasized the uniqueness and symbolism of Berlin—one of the most significant and exciting cities in the world.

History came together for me in a unique and moving way in 1987, when I attended, as a member of the Los Angeles Mayor's Delegation, the 750-year celebration of Berlin. (Los Angeles and Berlin are sister cities.) There I sat, in the ultramodern International Conference Center of Berlin, a German-American representing a country that is just over two hundred years old, celebrating almost four times that many years of rich culture and history. I realized that I was proud to be a son of Berlin, yet equally proud of the country I call my home today and its remarkable accomplishments during a much shorter period of history.

It also highlighted that special place Berlin has in the hearts of thousands of people from around the world, who, by their presence at that special occasion, emphasized the importance of freedom and friendship in a place then divided by a cruel Wall and surrounded by barbaric barbed wire.

During the celebration, at a concert in the Berlin Philharmonic put on by the Los Angeles Symphony Orchestra, I talked briefly to Mayor Eberhard Diepken about Berlin's historic significance. He observed that Berlin was actually a very young city, and Germany a very young country when you consider that the democratic process literally changed the fiber of the city and the nation. Actually, he said, Berlin was only just over forty—but it took the experience of the past 750 years to make her that young again.

Germans like their homes—which are truly their castles—and work hard to make sure they reflect their sense of *Gemütlichkeit* and comfort. A lot of time is spent there, reading, listening to good music or conversation, and enjoying family functions and time with friends. Home expresses one's status and lifestyle. The types of furniture or brand names of appliances are important, highlighting another German characteristic, that of status consciousness.

Though generally very hospitable, Germans do not make friends quickly, only acquaintances at first. However, once a friendship is earned and established, it is for life—sincere and genuine.

An invitation to a German home is a compliment and a special gesture of friendship. It is also a time to take along a bouquet of flowers for the hostess to express one's appreciation. I remember that my house was always filled with flowers, either from our garden or because my father frequently brought them home for my mother. Guests, friends, or relatives brought flowers when they came over for *Kaffee und Kuchen* (afternoon coffee) or *zum Abendessen* (dinner). It's a wonderful custom, one which people here in the United States have become increasingly fond of, too.

Most Germans do not own a house. The majority live in apartments or town houses, and those who live in houses probably inherited them. Germans are not as mobile as Americans. It is common for a German to grow up in an area, continue to live and work there, and see his children do the same.

In building their homes and planning their cities, Germans have been through a long learning process. Today, they regard cities, city centers, and plazas as extensions of "home," the place where they spend most of their lives. Germans look at their living and working places in a holistic sense, paying attention to making the total living environment satisfying, extending from the house or apartment, the courtyard and the garden, to the streets, the local shops, and to the entire community.

Very conscious of the environment, Germans plan new city projects to exclude the automobile and include appropriate public transportation and increasing the numbers of areas for bicycles or pedestrians only. Architects now design "human" environments, with the result that urban areas are being repopulated and are once again becoming centers of social and cultural interaction.

A favorite form of relaxation in Germany dates back to when the Romans first discovered mineral springs in Germany and built baths around them. Today, a visit to a spa is almost an annual ritual for many Germans and visitors alike. There are about 250 German spas. Mineral-water and mud-bath spas, with their curative powers, help invigorate those who feel stressed as a result of

a demanding and competitive work environment or who just want to have fun. Some thirty seaside resorts on the coasts of the North and Baltic seas offer seawater drinking and inhalation cures. Other resorts feature no more than a pure and healthy climate. All resorts have facilities for swimming, riding, golf, tennis, concerts, theater-going, and dancing—an array of activities bound to contribute to the rejuvenation of those who participate.

German people also enjoy walking, biking, and a variety of sports, either as spectators or participants. Vacations often include sailing on the ocean or on one of Germany's many lakes, riding at one of the prestigious stables, flying, golf, or tennis on the red clay courts.

Many of the sports can only be exercised in a club, either as a member or with a letter of recommendation. Germans are highly competitive when it comes to sports, so it pays well to play to win.

Other popular sports not necessarily played in exclusive clubs include soccer, track, bike-racing, and car-racing. Being a German sports fan, though, does not always mean participating. Millions of Germans watch sports as a national relief therapy.

When I was old enough to learn tennis, my dad gave me one of his rackets with about one-third cut off on the handle, since German manufacturers then had not discovered the "junior" market. That's another German trait—when you don't have exactly what you need, improvise.

Later, I added soccer and track to my life. When my school team represented its district in the Berlin School Olympics, I stood in the historic Olympic Stadium and thought of the 1936 Olympic games. From my place on the 400-meter relay team, I looked around the stadium, filled with over one hundred thousand cheering young people, and wondered how it must have been when Jesse Owens broke the world record and won a victory for equality without prejudice in our world. For me, participating in the same stadium where Jesse Owens ran was a dream come true.

Not only sports fans but also gourmet food lovers can have a field day in Germany. One of the country's favorite pastimes is good food, great beer, and exquisite wines. Each region in Germany has its own specialty, from Bockwurst to herring filet to Knoedel, from beef roasted on a spit to venison—something for everyone's taste. More than two hundred different kinds of bread, thirty different kinds of rolls, no less than twelve hundred different kinds of pastries, and more than fifteen hundred types of sausages are all available in Germany.

If you are a lover of foods, the KaDeWe in Berlin is a must. Every time I visit, I go to the sixth floor of the KaDeWe, probably the

largest department store in Europe, and spend the larger portion of the day viewing and tasting mouth-watering German food and specialties from all over the world. There's nothing you cannot find there—from hundreds of different breads and cheeses to Russian caviar; from smoked pheasant to fresh venison and roast duck; from lobster and eel to a delicious multitude of desserts, accompanied by a huge selection of German wines and beers.

As I walk away from there, I realize we've come a long way. My mind takes me back to the past, to sitting around the table with my family—dimmed lights, windows blocked because of air raids—eating, would you believe, bread-and-raisin soup.

Today, German cuisine includes a wide range of foods. Health foods are prevalent, and home-baked bread has become popular again. However, most items on German restaurant menus are still genuine German cuisine—and plenty of it. Visitors are always amazed at the large number and variety of items that are available at even the smallest of restaurants.

Dinner in Germany can be a long experience—especially if, when you're done, you don't ask for the check. In Frankfurt last summer, when I impatiently summoned the *Geschäftsführer* (restaurant manager) to ask why I had no check, his polite response was, "I am sorry, sir, but you didn't *ask* for it." Germans are inclined to go strictly by the book.

On vacation with my family, when we stopped for lunches on the Autobahn, it was always *Wienerschnitzel und Bratkartoffeln,* (breaded veal cutlet and fried potatoes) for me—to the dismay of my father, who thought my taste in food was rather monotonous. Even now, at least one *Wienerschnitzel* is a must while in Germany.

The delight of a German pastry demands a good cup of German coffee. While the British are ceremonial about their tea, Germans love their coffee and make an art of preparing, drinking, and enjoying it. One of the nicest things about the ritual is the wonderful aroma of a freshly brewed cup of German coffee.

Of course, beer and wine also rank high on the list of German pleasures, and seldom is a German meal served without a good glass of wine or German beer. With more than four thousand different German beers, there is enough variety to suit almost everyone. All are still made according to the German Purity Law, dating back to 1516. It allows for the use only of hops, malt, yeast, and water in the brewing of beer, and forbids any additives.

A fine dinner in Germany is often topped with an after-dinner drink. While German wines and beers have a special reputation all over the world, the surprising variety of German after-dinner drinks is little known, but equally enjoyable.

As good food is a genuine German tradition, so are festivals. There are as many popular festivals in Germany as there are days in the year. Many of them take place on the same day in different parts of the country. There are historical festivals with period costumes, wine festivals, hunters' festivals, flower festivals, firework displays, folk festivals, music festivals, and—of course—carnivals. Nearly every German city and town has its own tradition. In Munich, it's the *Fasching* and the *Oktoberfest;* in Nürnberg, the *Weihnachtsmarkt;* in the Harz, *Walpurgus Night;* and in Hameln, the legend of the Pied Piper is celebrated. At all these events you will find a great number of "merry people." As one German put it, "Here you meet a lot of friends you have never seen before in all your life."

There is also music everywhere in Germany—not just in the concert houses or opera halls. Germans grow up with music. I learned my first *Volkslied* in first grade and took music-appreciation classes through all my school years. When Germans get together for a good time, they also sing and dance. When they are tempted by wanderlust, their guitar goes along for great sing-along experiences around the campfire.

As my music teacher in high school once told me, borrowing the text of a *Volkskanon* (duet), "Heaven and earth might disappear, but the music, the music remains forever."

A description of German lifestyle would not be complete without a mention of the car. For Germans, a car is more than just a means of transportation. More often than not, that car is someone's pride and joy. Excellent highways crisscrossing the entire country offer ample opportunity to test one's sometimes most precious possession.

Driving in Germany, for me, will always be a wonderful experience. There's nothing like taking your car to its full potential—only to find out that, at 100 miles per hour, some other driver has passed you by as if you were standing still. I guess experiences like this are one of the reasons Germans appear to have steady nerves.

These days, standing still can be a wonderful experience, too. On a recent trip, I saw *Trabi* after *Trabi* (a nickname for the *Trabant,* East Germany's most common and notoriously temperamental car) stranded on the Autobahn. When I stopped and asked one East German family whether I could give any help, they responded, "No, it's okay. We'll get it started again. We don't really mind being stuck here, because now at least we're stuck free. It's a wonderful feeling!"

History has written another epic chapter about Germany—another that will not be forgotten. It is about freedom and the peaceful will of the people of Germany to be as one and to live as one.

Germany, situated in the heart of Europe, considers itself an integrated part of the European community and has assumed a leadership role in helping to create "a continent without borders." It has also become a driving force in this unification process, envisioning a combined future of all European countries, politically and culturally.

As a member of the United Nations, Germany has developed a strong foreign policy supporting the efforts of other nations to secure worldwide peace, economic and social progress, the implementation of human rights, and the right of self-determination of nations. It strongly condemns all kinds of racism and colonialism and gives determined resistance to the creation of new spheres of power and influence.

A jubilant nation as the result of the almost overnight transformation of East and West Germany into one Federal Republic of Germany on the third of October 1990, Germany once again is confronted with rebuilding.

Remembering that out of the ashes of World War II Germany created a proud new democracy with the strength, character, and initiative to renew itself, Germans swiftly grasped the opportunity for a fresh start. The results are evident everywhere. Success stories are bountiful. Germany is once again a respected partner in the international community.

Looking back, Germans have never forgotten that if it had not been for the Americans, British, and French and their generous sense of forgiveness and support for those who were once their enemies, Germany would not be where it is today. That healing gesture restored the self-confidence of a people once led, and gone, astray. Now Germany celebrates with open borders, open hearts, and open arms another new beginning for a Germany that is truly one nation.

But it will be almost as difficult to align the Eastern part of Germany with the standard of living and democratic freedom West Germans have enjoyed for so long as it was to rebuild after the war. Even though the Eastern part of Germany does not rise out of the ashes of war, it nevertheless rises out of the ashes of a cruel, limiting, politically and economically misguided, impersonal system that proves to be more difficult to overcome. There is a different mentality, a different educational background, a different value system.

That system made many people live a pretense. As one East German put it, most people in the East considered themselves "radishes." "When you cut one, you see what I mean," he said, "a fine layer of red on the outside and the rest all white."

The times to pretend are over. Persecution and fear exist no longer—but the memory lingers, and it will continue to linger for years. Once more, it is up to the German people, individually and collectively, to pull themselves out of the tragedy of the past. They must, with patience, hold the hands of their fellow Germans in the West as they held those of the Americans, British, and French, who, after the war, helped them restore their strength and belief in themselves.

To commemorate the collapse of the Berlin Wall and the regime which put it there, the renowned Leonard Bernstein conducted Beethoven's Ninth Symphony, "Ode to Joy," in the *Schauspielhaus* in East Berlin. Musicians and singers from the Soviet Union, the United States, France, Britain, Dresden, Munich, and Berlin joined in the celebration of freedom in a langauge that knows no borders—music.

Calling it "Ode to Freedom," with "freedom" substituted for "joy" throughout Friedrich von Schiller's soaring lines, it became an expression of joy such as has seldom been witnessed anywhere.

> "O friends, no more these sounds!
> Let us sing more cheerful songs,
> more full of joy (freedom)!"

For people there, and for those who watched the concert across the world, there was a feeling of global oneness, universal peace and friendship, along with a sense of gratefulness as expressed in Schiller's verse. After the concert, there was a quiet shout all over Germany, "Freedom reigns!" *Es lebe die Freiheit!*

Today, more than ever before, Germans can truly unite as a people and together sing Franz Joseph Haydn's beautiful melody— their national anthem:

> "Unity and right and freedom
>   for the German Fatherland,
> For this let us all fraternally
>   strive each with heart and hand.
> Unity and right and freedom
>   are the pledge of happiness.
> Bloom in the splendor of this happiness,
>   Germany, our Fatherland."

A clock face accentuates St. Jakob's tower, one of the six spires that dominate Hamburg's skyline. Rising 417 feet, this Gothic church was built in the thirteenth century; its organ, in 1693. ▶

Rügen, in East Germany, is the country's largest island in the sea. A paradise for sailing enthusiasts, it is also one of the most scenic and picturesque places off the Baltic coast. The island is connected to the mainland and to the city of Stralsund only by a sandway. ◄ Swans are a familiar sight in many parts of Germany. Near the island of Rügen, as the sun sets over the Baltic Sea, the swans portray solitude and tranquility. ▲

The Hanseatic town of Lübeck, famous for its marzipan, offers a scenic welcome to the evening visitor. Guarded by the Holstentor, which was built in 1477, the town retains much of its original splendor. It is one of the busiest ports on the Baltic Sea. ▲ A young German woman makes her way back from an afternoon shopping trip. Going shopping means easy walking within the central shopping district of the city. ▶

A farm woman stands proudly in front of the colorful entrance to her home in Altesland. ◄ The horse is still a major "power" in farming, especially in the area that was once East Germany. Team effort and friendship between man and horse, *Mann und Pferd,* have been the tradition for centuries in the rural areas. Rügen's landscape is mixed—including farmland, nature preserves, and gardens filled with holly and orchids. ▲

Gigantic cranes reach into the evening skies of the busy port of Hamburg. Visited regularly by more than three hundred shipping lines, the port handles cargo bound for a thousand destinations worldwide. ▲ Hamburg is alive at night. Lit by colorful neon lights that reflect in the calm waters of the Alster, it offers an abundance of entertainment, fine restaurants, and German pubs for residents and visitors alike. ▶ A walk along the Alster on a warm summer evening is colorful and romantic. ▶ ▶

In Bremen's city center, modern transportation contrasts with architecture dating back to A.D. 965. The oldest maritime city in Germany, Bremen ranks second only to Hamburg as an international German port. It began trading with the United States in 1783. ▲ A heron looks out to sea from the shores of the fishing and resort village of Warnemünde in East Germany. The town is known for its charming lighthouse, old brick fishermen's houses, sandy beaches, and colorful fishing boats. ▶

It is a legend of Germany that the stork brings good luck to newlyweds. When storks are seen nesting on a chimney or church steeple, expectant parents make a wish for a boy or a girl. According to the folk tale, the stork carries the baby, bundled in cloth filled with hay, to its new home and drops it down the chimney. ◄ Pigs are a major commodity in Germany, valued for cuisine and export. Though *Schwein* is the German word for "pigs," it also stands for "dirty." This Schleswig-Holstein champion is spic-and-span clean — a definite paradox, especially for Germany. ▲

Aglow in the fire of the setting
sun, this Schleswig-Holstein farmhouse nestles beside dense woods,
which protect it from threatening seawinds and storms. ▲ A church
tower dominates the country around a Schleswig-Holstein village. ▶

An East German shepherd takes time out to show off a handmade shoulder belt. ◄ A picturesque, wooded countryside surrounds an autumn forest near Kassel. The town was the home of the Brothers Grimm, who, in the early 1800s, wrote and compiled an array of children's tales. Surroundings such as these could certainly furnish the inspiration for fairy tales. ▲

Hamburg is called the "Venice of the North" because of its many canals, waterways, and bridges. The Köhlbrandbrücke Bridge, set against the evening sky, is a marvel of modern engineering. ▲ This is a typical Lüneburger house. The region is the most beautiful during August, when the heather is in bloom, and the birches, pines, and junipers are in leaf. ▶

HEINRICH BLEEKEN ❦ MINNA BLEEKEN GEB. TÖDTER ❦ ANNO 1949

West of Hamburg, in marshy Altesland, stands a typical, decorative half-timbered farmhouse. Known for its delicious apples and cherries, Altesland is a good area for walks along rivers and canals. ◄ "Strong in mind and body" is the trademark of the women of former East Germany who work the fields of once cooperatively or state owned farmland. The character of the working women in Germany emerged from the groups of women in the post-war era who worked among ashes and rubble to clean up and set the foundations for reconstruction of their cities. ▲

A paradise of sea, sun, and sand, the Frisian island of Sylt is in the North Sea. Sylt, famous for its fine sand, is often referred to as the St. Tropez of the north. ▲ "A man's house is his castle" is literally true in Germany. Passed down from generation to generation, a house is the expression of a family's pride. In Stade, a museum that was once a home provides a good example of German respect for the historic. ▶ Former East Germany's largest seaside resort on the Baltic Sea, Warnemünde is dotted with rows of *Strandkörbe,* wicker chairs for two. ▶ ▶

St. Catherine's rises 367 feet in the air above the tugboats of Hamburg harbor. The church, built in the thirteenth and fourteenth centuries, combines Gothic and baroque architectural styles. ◄ Numerous rivers, lakes, and canals provide habitat for swans. Feeding them bread crumbs is a common German pastime. ▲ Spring is a *Stilleben,* a "still-life" of beauty of a special kind, when the trees blossom and fields fill with color. ► ►

Love and pride radiate from the face of a German farm woman holding her chicken, as she rests on the garden bench next to her brick house. ▲ A quaint fishing town on the North Sea coast lights up in the late afternoon sun. ▶

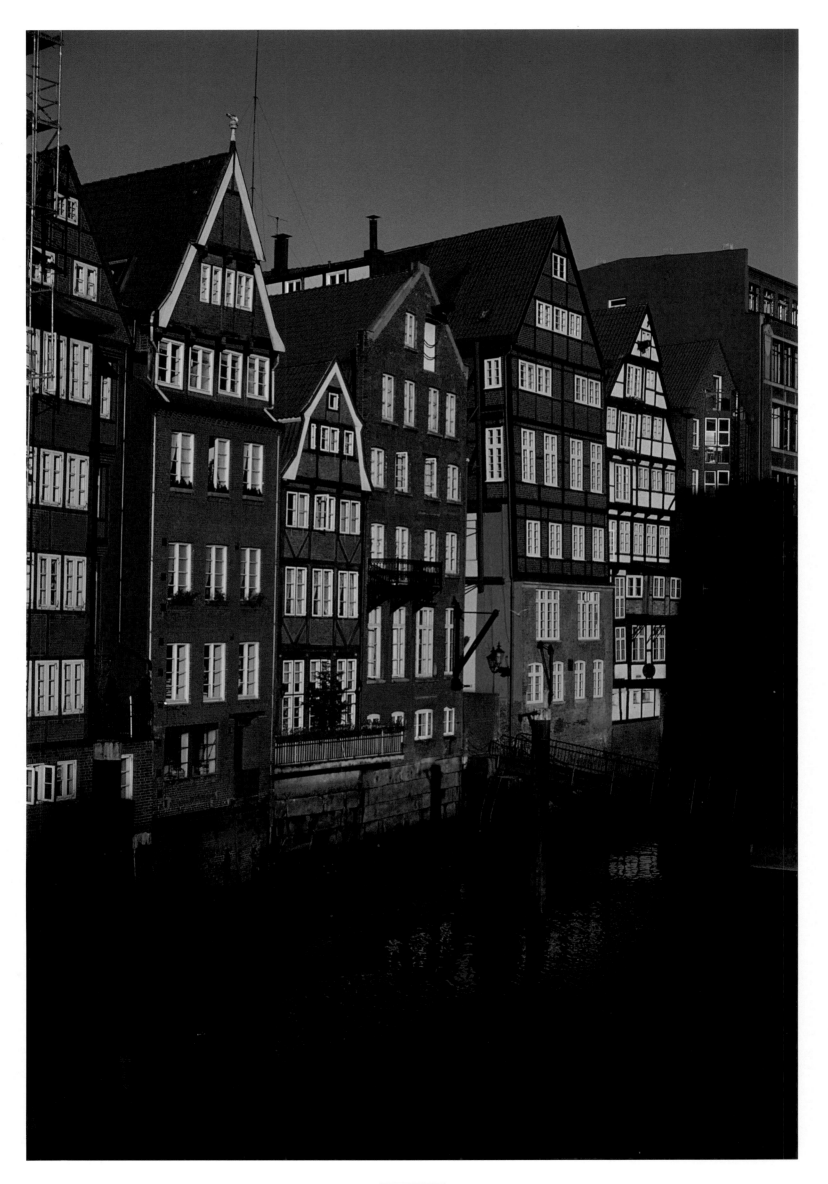

Along Diechstrasse, a famous old
street in Hamburg, century-old merchant houses line the water-
front. ◄ The Alster, in Hamburg's center, is a favorite site for sailing
enthusiasts, who sail for pleasure or in one of the annual regattas. ▲

Standing on an island in a lake, the ninth-century Castle Schwerin reflects Gothic, baroque, and Renaissance styles. A nearby park adds charm to the unique castle, which was modeled after the Chambord Castle in France. ▲ This Russian war memorial, guarded by Russian honor guards, is located in what was once West Berlin. Dedicated to unknown soldiers, it has been a monument of war, peace, and East-West confrontation. ▶

The festive nineteenth-century Semper Opera House, Dresden

A city of galleries and museums, Dresden is a showplace of art, inside and out, as can be seen alongside the walls of this historic building, where intricate murals tell stories of years past. ▲ Reflected on the surface of its surrounding lake, Castle Moritzburg dominates the countryside near Dresden. ▶

The East German medieval township of Bautzen

Everywhere, German cities are full of fountains, ranging from the historic to the modern, from the simple to the intricate. This fountain at the Karl Marx Plaza in Leipzig displays fine copper and marble artwork. ◄ A center for both the bookselling and printing trades, Leipzig is home to the *Leipziger Messe,* the largest trade fair in Eastern Europe. Leipzig is also rich with museums. The outstanding Leipzig Art Museum, shown here in evening glow, is one of the city's finest examples. ▲

A typical autumn forest in central Germany

Through the decades, Frankfurt, Germany's financial capital, has restored its city center. With combined tradition and innovation, the city's old street lights contrast with the impressive headquarters of Deutsche Bank, the major banking institution in Germany. ▲ At Degussa, Germany's premier precious metals company, the shining reflections of the pure gold ingots (2.2046 pounds each) emerge from a sea of gold nuggets. ▶

Christmas brightens hearts and faces all over Germany, and tradition stirs in every market square. One of the most famous markets is in Frankfurt, where the center of the Altestadt is lit up, and holiday foods and handcrafted wares and gifts are sold in tents. ◄ *Deutsche Lufthansa* means "German air fleet." Frankfurt is the major gateway for Lufthansa German Airlines, which displays as its logo the proud *Kranich,* or crane. ▲

Concrete and a bicyclist contrast with flowing water, creating a silhouette of simple beauty at the Opernplatz in front of the Frankfurt Opera House. ▲ The opera house, Alte Oper, has been rebuilt to its original splendor. First opened in 1880, it was destroyed in 1944 and reopened in 1981. ▶ Frankfurt, home to more than 350 international banks, has developed a skyline rivaling many of those in the United States. ▶ ▶

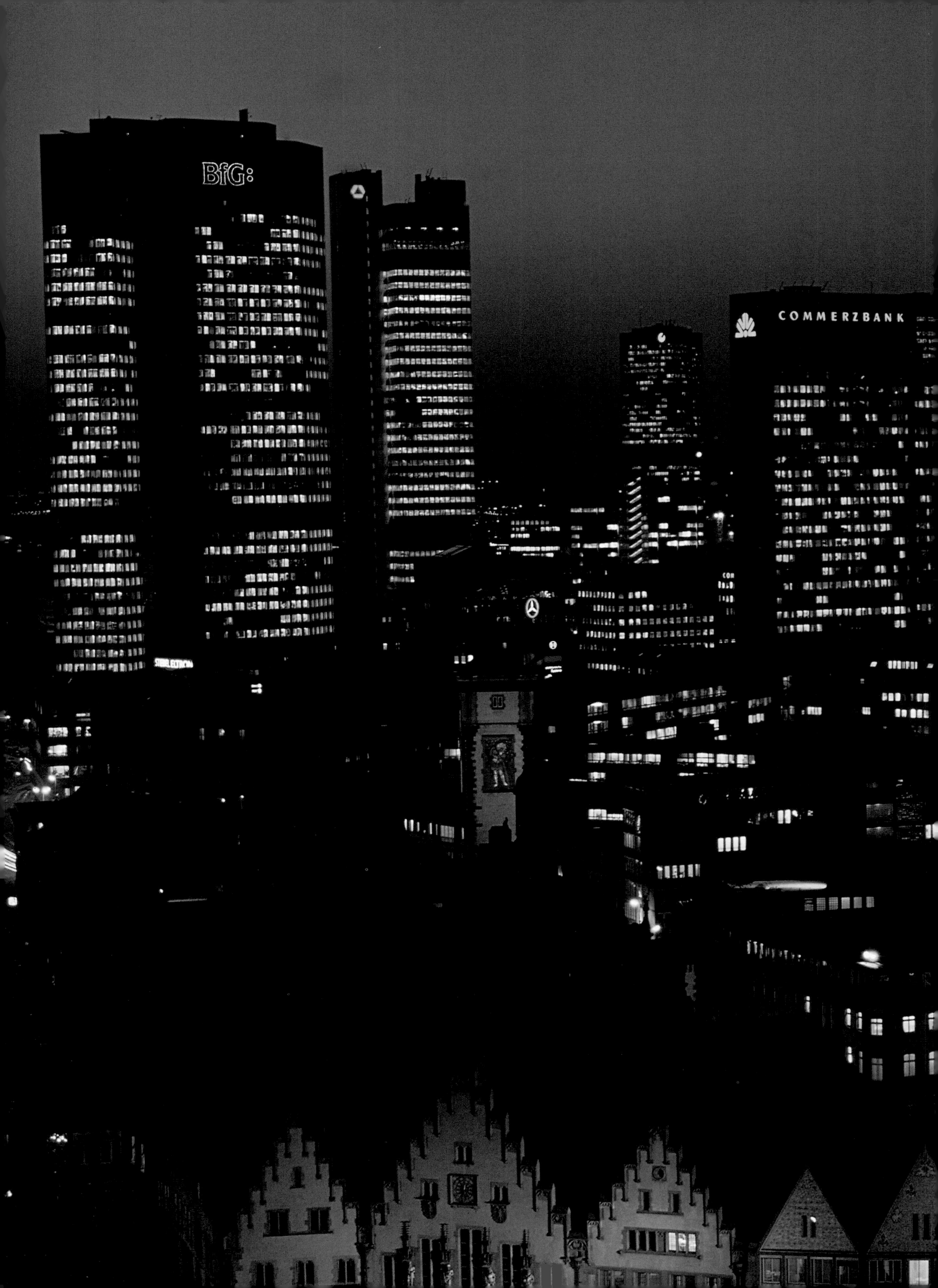
BfG:
COMMERZBANK

The Marienberg citadel, nestled among vineyards, towers over Würzburg at the Main River. Built during the twelfth and thirteenth centuries, it became an imperial fortress during the seventeenth century. Today, it contains magnificent replicas of the past. ◄ The Lahn River flows by one of the most picturesque villages in the world. Runkel Castle, built right into the rock, overlooks the fifteenth-century town and offers a panoramic view of Taunus and Westerwald. ▲ Freudenberg in the Sauerland displays its carefully restored, historic town center. ► ►

St. Koloman, near Füssen, stands as a beacon of faith in the shadows of the Bavarian Alps. ▲ Puppet theatres are a common sight in German villages. Performing as characters in medieval fairy tales, the handcrafted puppets tell stories of the past. ▶ The town clock overlooks the city square from a rooftop in Dinkelsbühl alongside the Romantic Road. This medieval town still has its original watchtowers and ramparts. ▶ ▶

In a veritable *winter Wunderland,*
ice-coated branches stand out against an azure sky before a small
Bavarian village. ◄　A rising winter sun awakens the Alpine land. ▲
Morning mists hover over the village of Sankt Urban, where rich,
green pastures climb up to the majestic and breathtaking Alps. ► ►

Red poppies, found throughout many parts of Germany, attract the bees that produce the country's honey. ◄ Overlooking Wörmitz Valley alongside Romantic Road, the fortified castle of Harburg evokes a fairy-tale mood. The brilliant red poppy fields surrounding the castle add to the effect. ▲

This Mercedes-Benz star hood ornament, the well-known corporate logo of Daimler-Benz, is a symbol of German engineering, advanced technology, and precision. ▲ Since medieval times, artisans have been known by the beautifully crafted signs they have used outside their establishments to identify themselves and their trades. Here, a polished bell at the *Gasthof* invites you to a rustic meal or an overnight stay. ▶

In Bavaria's medieval Dinkelsbühl on the Romantic Road, children dress in colorful costumes to pay tribute to their country's survival of the Thirty Years' War. ◄ In Munich, the people celebrate Oktoberfest, a traditional festival which is held each year during the second half of September. ▲

An Eastern Allgäu landscape with snow, blue skies, and mountains

A woman holds her favorite pet rabbit in the yard of her Bavarian farmhouse. ▲ Churches such as this, typical to Bavarian townships, play a central role in the architecture and the traditional lifestyle of these communities. ▶

A church, trees, and a cross are silhouetted against the sky in Schongau along the Romantic Road in southern Bavaria. ◄ A friendly cow, such as this one, is a common living landmark of the Allgäu region. The famous Alpine milk is used throughout Germany in exquisite chocolates and cheeses. ▲

Nature seems untouched by the encroachments of mankind in the hilly woods of the Alps. Here, wildlife is preserved to keep natural balance in the region. ▲ A visit to Rothenburg ob der Tauber is a step back to the twelfth century. Completely intact with fortified walls and towers, Rothenburg, a showcase of medieval life, is a favorite Romantic Road sight. ▶

Bavaria's Highway 16 offers numerous vistas along the Danube.

Neuschwanstein Castle stands sentinel over a dreamy, magical countryside scene in Bavaria. ◄ The Zugspitze, rising behind a Bavarian church and farm, is the highest peak in the German Alps. ▲ Rugged Alpine mountains rise in the background and storm clouds descend in the late afternoon skies as a lone windsurfer on the Hopfensee rides the waters. ► ►

A smile and a glass of Bavarian beer go hand in hand as a sun-weathered villager makes a toast to good health, to his friends, and to the rest of the world. ▲ Breads, sausages, and cheeses are essential to the menus of Bavarian restaurants. ▶ The moon shines above the skyline of Munich. ▶ ▶

In Dinkelsbühl, women pause in their gardening for a friendly chat. A vegetable garden is maintained outside the city by volunteers, providing nutritious food for the needy. ◄ People from all over the world gather in the tents of Munich's Oktoberfest. Sitting on benches with arms interlocked, they sing along to the band's Bavarian tunes. Approximately ten million pints of beer, seven hundred thousand sausages, and seven hundred fifty thousand chickens are devoured during the festival. ▲

Hundreds of rides and entertainments, along with special foods, are part of the celebration called Oktoberfest. ▲ This southern German boy proudly wears the attire of his region—lederhosen and a hunter's hat. The leather pants, also popular in other parts of Germany because they are so practical, are virtually indestructible—they can only be outgrown. ▶

The Alpine region is a veritable skier's paradise. Locals seem to be "born with their skis on," and visitors enjoy the runs and slopes available—not to forget Bavaria's famous *après-ski* life, an evening of candlelit relaxation after a day of skiing. ◄ The silhouettes of trees rise out of the silvery snow into the golden purple evening glow of an Alpine countryside. ▲

Spring flowers brighten the farm-land beside the road leading to a remote Bavarian homestead. ▲ In Regensburg, the twin towers of St. Peter's Gothic cathedral, which dates back to the thirteenth century, rise majestically above the Danube River. The spikes were added in the nineteenth century. ▶

As the sun sets over Rothenburg ob der Tauber, the picturesque medieval town is veiled by a sea of mist. ◄ A tropical paradise amidst Alpine scenery, the island of Mainau stands in Lake Constance, which is Germany's southern-most lake. The high altitude and protective mountain surroundings of Austria, Switzerland, and Germany create a gentle climate. ▲

Altensteig, typical of many Black Forest villages

Portraying an old folk tale, a handcrafted ornament on a Black Forest tavern and brewery bids welcome to guests. ◄ A Black Forest farmhouse, a combination of house and barn, almost fades into the slope it is built on and the trees surrounding it. The building overlooks rich, rolling farmland. ▲

In Freiburg, farmers from surrounding areas bring their fresh produce, flowers, and other wares to market. German homemakers prefer to shop in these farmers' markets where they are assured of quality and freshness. ▲ Apples are a specialty crop in many parts of Germany. Sold all over Europe, the apples have a mouth-watering, "give-me-another-apple" flavor. ▶

The Castle Lichtenstein reigns over the Swabian Alps of Baden-Württemberg, near Echaz Valley. Built on top of a rock formation, it was once a formidable small fortress. ◄ The pilgrim church of Birnau stands on the shores of Lake Constance, "the Swabian Sea." Worshippers enjoy the serenity of its interior as well as the grandeur of its surroundings—from the vast beauty of the lake to the monumental splendor of the Alps. ▲

With the background sound of rushing water, this century-old mill and the colorful hanging flowers create a picture-perfect scene for a fairy tale. ▲ St. Goar, at the foot of Rheinfels Castle on the River Rhine, is the setting for this exquisite *Kuckucksuhr,* considered the world's largest free-hanging cuckoo clock. Handcrafted of fine wood and colorfully painted, not only is its time accurate, but it also is a masterpiece of craftsmanship. ▶

An architectural mosaic of color, wood, metal, caulk, and shingles presents itself on a clock *Giebel,* or gable, at Urach's town hall. One of the most picturesque small towns in the Swabian Alps, Urach is nestled deep in the Erms River Valley. ◄ Morning awakens the pastures, the wooded hills, and the waters of the Rhineland region as the sun slowly dispels the mists. ▲

Vineyards, the River Rhine, and Castle Stahleck

A cluster of Riesling grapes is
silhouetted against the late summer sun. Fine Riesling wines have
made the Rhine, Mosel, and Neckar regions famous worldwide. ◄
The renowned Castle Cochem overlooks the town of Cochem at the
Mosel River, a favorite wine-tasting area. The hills are covered with
vineyards which produce some of the finest wines in Germany. ▲

Famous for its cathedral, built over six centuries, Cologne symbolizes perseverance and reverence for God. Reaching for the heavens, the intricately detailed Gothic cathedral evokes wonder and awe. ▲ The cathedral stands beside other dramatically lit historic sites, as the skyline is reflected on the Rhine. This is also a site of special festivities, including the famous annual Cologne Carnival and the Corpus Christi procession. ▶

Emerging from a green marsh dotted with spring flowers, a wooden windmill rises into the stormy skies of Friesland. ◄ With beautiful poppies growing freely on one side of a dividing fence, Nature is an unknowing symbol of the way Germans looked at West and East before unification. ▲

Hard work and determination have made the *Marschen,* or marshes, of Friesland fertile. They are now successfully cultivated, despite storms and the battering of the seas. ▲ A Friesland home and its entrance show clear signs of the influence of the neighboring Netherlands on style and color. ▶

In Friesland, a chicken confers with its fellow cats about the duties for the day on the steps of a farmhouse entrance. ◄ The silhouettes of tree windbreakers on the flatland of Friesland stand out against a colorful sunset. ▲

Ich mochte besonders danken: Mike Tauchel, meinem Freund aus Rostock, welcher meine Arbeit in Ostdeutschland viel leichter machte, Hans Jilka aus Altenstadt und auch ein grossartiger Fotograf fuer seine Freundschaft, Simon Pettrich und seiner Frau fuer mein Miethaus welches es moeglich machte, mir und meiner Familie in Deutschland kompfortabel zu wohnen, meinen Freunden aus Repperfoto in Schongau fuer super Service und die Filmentwicklungen, meinem Freund Ingo Brand und seinen Eltern aus Stade fuer mehrere schoene Wochen Unterkunft und leztendlich meinem Sohn, Justin, und meiner Frau, Valerie, fuer das Teilen der Abenteuer. Noch einmal, vielen Dank Euch allen fuer die Erinnerungen.

I would like to especially thank Mike Tauchel, my friend from Rostock which made my work in East Germany much easier; Hans Jilka from Altenstadt, also a great photographer, for his friendship; Simon Pettrich and his wife for the rental house in Schongau, which allowed my family and me to have a comfortable stay; my friends at Repperfoto in Schongau for their super service and great film processing; my friend Ingo Brand and his parents in Stade for several memorable weeks; and, lastly, of course, my son Justin and my wife Valerie for sharing in the adventure. Once again, many thanks to each one of you for your great support.

BRYAN F. PETERSON

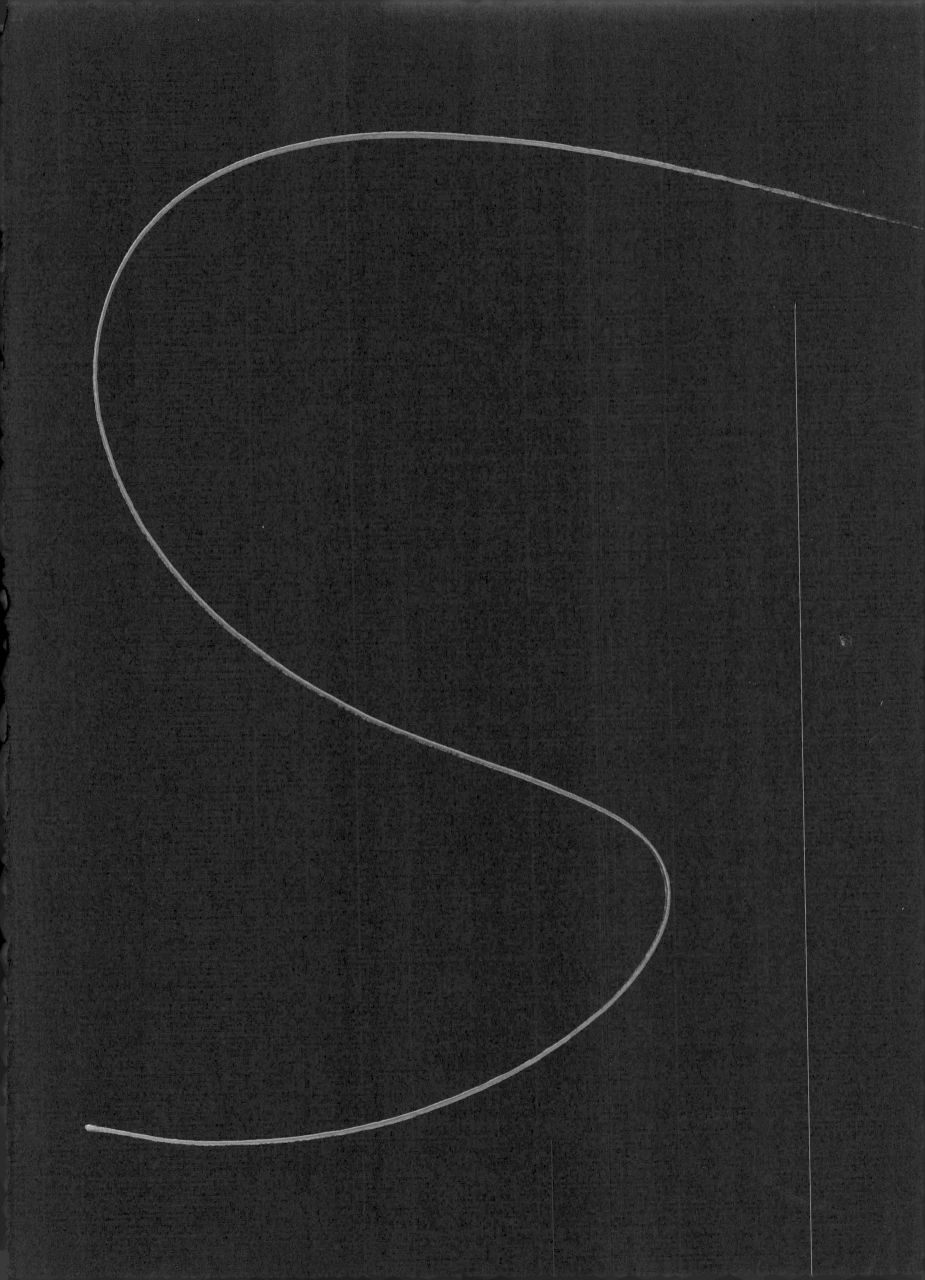